Animal Teams

Penguin Colonies

by Lisa Bullard

FOCUS READERS®

BEACON

www.focusreaders.com

Focus Readers is distributed by North Star Editions:
sales@northstareditions.com | 888-417-0195

Produced for Focus Readers by Red Line Editorial.

Photographs ©: Shutterstock Images, cover, 1, 4, 6, 8, 11, 12, 18, 20, 22, 24, 29; iStockphoto, 14–15, 16, 26

Library of Congress Cataloging-in-Publication Data
Names: Bullard, Lisa, author.
Title: Penguin colonies / by Lisa Bullard.
Description: Mendota Heights, MN: Focus Readers, [2025] | Series: Animal teams | Includes bibliographical references and index. | Audience: Grades 2-3
Identifiers: LCCN 2023054175 (print) | LCCN 2023054176 (ebook) | ISBN 9798889981930 (hardcover) | ISBN 9798889982494 (paperback) | ISBN 9798889983583 (pdf) | ISBN 9798889983057 (ebook)
Subjects: LCSH: Penguins--Juvenile literature | Penguins--Behavior--Juvenile literature | Penguins--Life cycles--Juvenile literature
Classification: LCC QL696.S473 B85 2025 (print) | LCC QL696.S473 (ebook) | DDC 598.47--dc23/eng/20231220
LC record available at https://lccn.loc.gov/2023054175
LC ebook record available at https://lccn.loc.gov/2023054176

Printed in the United States of America
Mankato, MN
082024

About the Author

Lisa Bullard is the author of more than 100 books for children, including the mystery novel *Turn Left at the Cow*. She also teaches writing classes for adults and children. Lisa grew up in Minnesota and now lives just north of Minneapolis.

Table of Contents

Chapter 1

Sticking Together

The king penguin chick is six weeks old. His mother and father just left. They are hunting food for him. But the chick is not alone. He joined a **crèche**. Other chicks are around.

Baby king penguins have fluffy brown feathers.

The middle of a huddle is the safest place for a chick.

On cold days, the chicks move closer to one another. They **huddle** together to keep warm. They stay safe, too. Their **predators** often avoid chicks in groups.

Finally, the chick's parents return. They approach the **colony**. The colony has thousands of babies. But the parents know their chick's call. They find him again.

The chick has not eaten for three months. At last, it's time for food. The chick gulps down the bits of fish and shrimp.

Penguins are born on land or ice. But their food comes from the sea.

Chapter 2

Penguin Families

Most penguins are **social** animals. They live together in large colonies. Some colonies are on land. Others are on sea ice. In each colony, families spend time together.

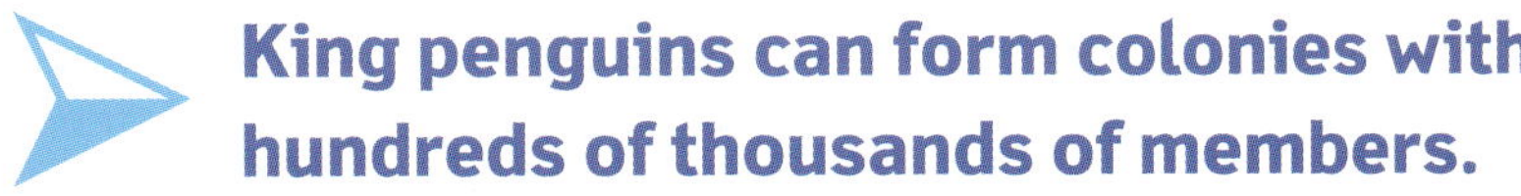

King penguins can form colonies with hundreds of thousands of members.

When penguins grow up, they look for **mates**. Males and females go back to where they were born. Thousands of penguins from the colony are there. That makes it easy to find a mate.

After mating, females lay one or two eggs. Protecting an egg is not easy. So, the parents work together. Many parents take turns warming the egg. They also trade jobs. One penguin guards the egg. The other looks for food. Then, they switch.

Hatching time varies for different penguins. It takes about a month for erect-crested penguins.

The parents keep trading until the egg hatches. That can take a month or more.

More than 150,000 pairs of king penguins come together in St. Andrews Bay.

After eggs hatch, many parents continue their teamwork. One keeps the chick safe. The other hunts. They feed the baby and change places again.

When the chick is old enough, parents can leave it with the colony. Then both parents can hunt. After a year, most chicks are fully grown. They can find their own food. Soon, each penguin can find a mate, too. They can start their own families. The colony can keep growing.

Some penguins use rocks to build nests. They might steal rocks from neighbors in the colony.

THAT'S AMAZING!

Fathers Huddle

Most penguins live in cold areas. Emperor penguins lay eggs during freezing Antarctic winters. Mothers leave to find food. Fathers care for the eggs.

Each father holds an egg in a pouch near his feet. Groups of fathers huddle together for warmth. But penguins on the outside get cold. So, the huddle shifts. Each penguin takes small steps. Their movements turn the group around. Warmer penguins go to the edges. Colder penguins slip inside. Teamwork keeps everyone warm.

Emperor penguins hold babies at their feet after they hatch.

Chapter 3

Hunting Helpers

Penguins eat animals such as fish, **krill**, and squid. They hunt for these animals in the water. Many penguins hunt in groups. Galápagos penguins do this. So do Humboldt penguins.

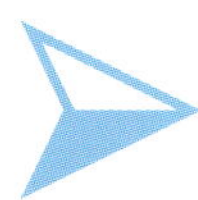

Penguins eat many types of fish, including anchovies, cod, and silverfish.

A group of penguins moves through the water, searching for food.

Penguins use their eyesight to find food. But **prey** can be hard to see in the ocean. Group hunting makes the job easier. If one penguin spots food, it lets the others know. Everyone knows where to look.

Penguins use several **methods** to catch food. One way is herding. That's when many penguins force other animals to move in a group.

African penguins often herd fish. While swimming, they push groups of fish together. That makes it easier to catch the fish. The penguins can grab several fish at once. They can catch fish that try to escape, too.

Chinstrap penguins may swim 50 miles (80 km) offshore each day to find food.

Synchronized diving is another way to catch food. First, the penguins form hunting groups on land. Then they move into the water together. Each penguin dives at the same time. Chinstrap penguins use this method. They mostly dive to catch krill. The penguins dive together. And each penguin gets a similar amount of food. Their teamwork helps make the hunt successful.

Penguins do not have teeth. Spines in their mouths help them grab food. Then they swallow their food whole.

Chapter 4

Predator Protection

Penguins are great hunters. But they can be hunted, too. Adult penguins sometimes face danger on land. Animals such as foxes and snakes hunt some penguins.

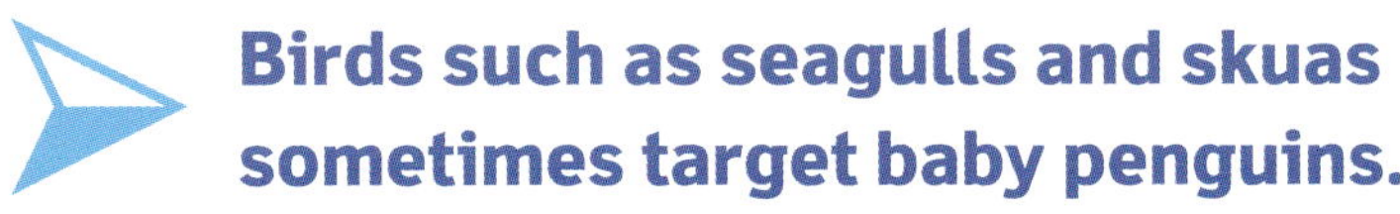

Adélie penguins dive into the water one after another.

Baby penguins and eggs face the most danger. Some flying birds eat them. So, many penguins build their nests close together. Predators might fly in to grab a chick or egg.

But angry adult penguins can respond. Together, they fight off the predators.

Penguins face predators in the water, too. Animals such as seals and killer whales might eat them. A lone swimming penguin is a great target. But a predator can't catch several penguins at once. Like on land, penguins often stick together in the water. For example, Adélie penguins dive together. A group starts out standing on the ice.

Some penguins can move fast enough to look like they are flying along the water's surface.

One penguin dives into the water. The next one quickly follows. Soon the whole group has joined. That helps them stay safe.

Moving in groups also helps penguins stay **alert**. That's because there are more penguins to notice if danger is near. If one penguin spots a predator, it warns the colony. The penguin uses a loud sound to announce the danger. Then the others can hide or rush away.

Penguins use many different sounds to share information. Danger calls sound different from mating calls.

FOCUS ON

Penguin Colonies

Write your answers on a separate piece of paper.

1. Write a few sentences explaining some activities penguins do together.
2. Do you think it's harder for penguins to guard eggs or hunt for food? Why?
3. What is a group of baby penguins that sticks together called?
   - A. a crèche
   - B. a nest
   - C. a predator
4. Why do young penguins face more danger than grown penguins?
   - A. Young penguins taste better to predators.
   - B. Young penguins can't fight back.
   - C. Young penguins are always alone.

5. What does **synchronized** mean in this book?

Synchronized *diving is another way to catch food. First, the penguins form hunting groups on land. Then they move into the water together. Each penguin dives at the same time.*

A. done in the same way together
B. done in many different ways
C. done very slowly

6. What does **lone** mean in this book?

A ***lone*** *swimming penguin is a great target. But a predator can't catch several penguins at once.*

A. fast
B. very big
C. by itself

Answer key on page 32.

Glossary

alert
Ready to notice danger and react quickly.

colony
A group of animals that live together.

crèche
A group of penguin chicks gathered together.

huddle
To crowd together.

krill
Small animals that float in the sea and look similar to shrimp.

mates
Animals that pair off to create young.

methods
Ways to do something.

predators
Animals that hunt other animals for food.

prey
Animals that are hunted by other animals for food.

social
Likely to spend time with other animals of the same type.

To Learn More

BOOKS

Bolte, Mari. *I Am Not a Penguin: Animals in the Polar Regions*. North Mankato, MN: Capstone Press, 2023.

DK Super Readers Level 3: Emperor Penguins. New York: DK Publishing, 2023.

Jaycox, Jaclyn. *Penguins Are Awesome*. North Mankato, MN: Capstone Press, 2020.

NOTE TO EDUCATORS

Visit **www.focusreaders.com** to find lesson plans, activities, links, and other resources related to this title.

Index

Answer Key: 1. Answers will vary; **2.** Answers will vary; **3.** A; **4.** B; **5.** A; **6.** C